PIA'S JOURNEY TO THE HOLY LAND

PIA'S JOURNEY TO THE HOLY LAND

Story and pictures by
SVEN AND PIA GILLSÄTER

HARCOURT, BRACE & WORLD, INC.
NEW YORK

FIRST PUBLISHED IN SWEDEN IN 1960 UNDER THE TITLE OF
PIAS RESA I HELIGA LANDET

TRANSLATED FROM THE SWEDISH BY ANNABELLE MACMILLAN

PRINTED IN GERMANY BY ORT OFFSETDRUCK KONSTANZ

Looking at a Christmas crèche, millions of children have dreamed of the real meaning behind the words of the story that begins: "And it came to pass in those days..." (*Luke 2:1*) Pia's dream came true.

The plane took off, and everything below grew smaller. Houses and trees became miniatures; even the Alps turned into tiny toy mountains. At last Pia was on her way to the land of the Christmas crèche. While the motors of the plane droned on, she began to wonder what she would see when she got there. It was such a long trip — much longer than she had imagined.

Palestine was called the Holy Land, she knew, because Jesus had been born and lived there. But could they all be real—the things she had read about in the Bible, the stories that the grownups had told her? What would a

holy land look like? Were there still shepherds in this country, shepherds who tended their flocks with long crooks in their hands? And were there still Wise Men, like the three who had traveled so far to Bethlehem, the city where Jesus was born?

Pia knew also that the land of the Bible is now divided into two parts. Not too long ago one half, which is called Israel, became once more the Land of the Jews, and many of its present-day inhabitants have come from all corners of the world to the country that their forefathers at one time left.

The other half, called Jordan, is where the Arabs live. They have inhabited the land of the Bible for so long that they consider the whole of it their own. But now the border between the two countries runs straight through the town of Jerusalem — a none-too-friendly border, with its barbed wire and its soldiers on constant guard.

Night came as the plane flew over the Mediterranean, and the moon shone down on the sea. Pia fell into a deep and dreamless sleep.

When she awoke, she could see little but green and gold below: the earth and the stones, orange groves, and occasional small white houses. Suddenly a huge green field seemed to rush up toward her, and in a few minutes the plane landed on the airfield. So this was Israel! She looked all around and almost at once caught sight of the reddish-yellow hills and mountains over toward Bethlehem and Jerusalem.

This is El Al's giant plane, which has just landed in the Lydda airport between Tel Aviv and Jerusalem.

BETHLEHEM

It was Christmas Eve, and Pia was in Bethlehem! The bus came to a stop at a public square near the Church of the Nativity, which had been built over the stable where Jesus was born. The narrow streets teemed with people — black-bearded monks, nuns in white head-dresses, Arabs in red burnooses with black bands around their heads, tourists from all over the world. High above, the chime of church bells rang out.

Pia struggled up the steep steps leading to the tower of the Church of the Nativity. Through arched openings in

Bethlehem was and still is a small town, a few miles south of Jerusalem. It is a humble Eastern town, with narrow streets and flat roofs. But the star shone over it.

the walls she looked out over the city. The white houses were bathed in light, and high over the flat roofs towered the spires of Bethlehem's many mosques and churches. On one roof a cat lay sunning itself; on another a woman was doing her laundry.

Here in the tower Pia realized fully, for the first time, how different the new land was from her own. It was Christmas Eve, but there was no snow; there were no gifts and no Christmas trees. And yet right here, in the narrow streets below, the first Christmas had been celebrated. Here Jesus was born; here the Wise Men from

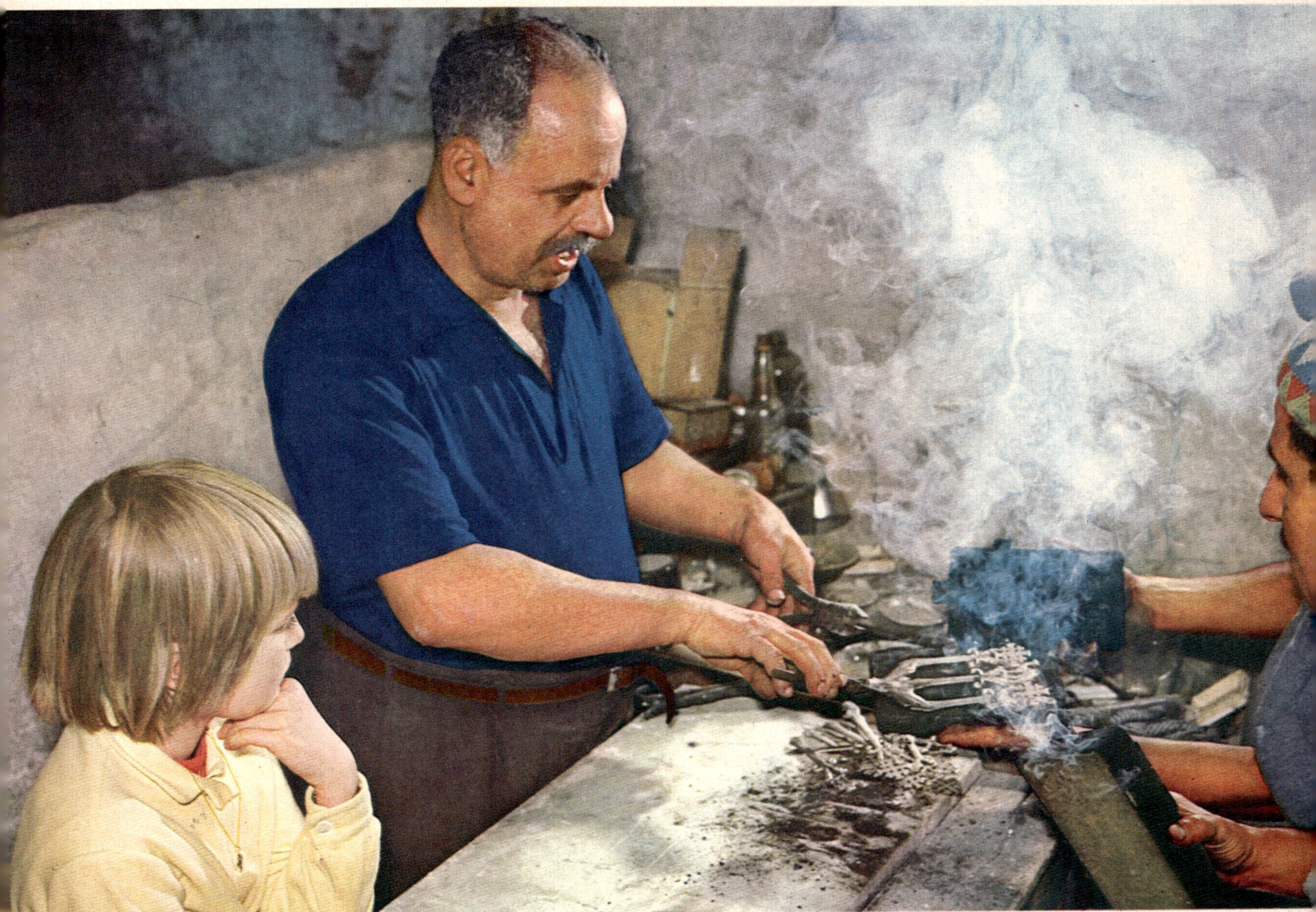

Above: Bethlehem is a city of craftsmen. Here the silversmith, Zachariah, is busy making small souvenirs of the place where Jesus was born.

Left: Even today shepherds travel to Jerusalem from the pastures of Judea. Nowadays they linger over gaudy movie advertisements with Arabic script, and the subject of greatest interest is American movie stars.

the East had come long ago, following the star that shone over Bethlehem.

Pia came down from the tower, went through the large church and down the cellar stairway. Soon she stood in a grotto where candles fluttered and oil lamps flickered. Pictures and matting hung on the walls, and it was very quiet under the rough stone ceiling. Almost two thousand years ago Mary and Joseph had come to this very place. It was here that Jesus was born, and all the Christmas crèches in the world are copies of this stone crib.

Outside in the city, darkness had begun to fall. In the motley crowd of people Pia was shoved hither and thith-

er, but everyone seemed friendly and happy. Eventually she came to a little square and was able to catch her breath. A ragged beggar went by with a long staff in his hand, and then a flock of bleating sheep. There were the shepherds she had wondered about so much. They wore long grayish robes and white headcloths, and they talked constantly among themselves.

The shepherds had come to Bethlehem to sell their sheep; once they received payment for their animals they planned to go to the movies. It seemed strange to Pia that anyone should go to the movies in Bethlehem, the city where Jesus was born, on Christmas Eve!

A narrow stone staircase leads to the grotto of the Nativity — the ruins of the stable where Joseph and Mary were forced to go when there was no room for them in the inn.

Today thousands of people come to see the town of Jesus' childhood, where donkeys are just as much a part of the traffic as are the tourist buses.

NAZARETH

Nazareth lies hemmed in among the treeless, stony hills of Galilee. Pia rode to the market place on a patient donkey. There were crowds of people, just as there had been in Bethlehem. Outside the shops, the merchandise had been put right on the stones of the street. In the midst of the crowds half-naked children scurried about at play.

Once upon a time, long ago, Jesus was one of those children, Pia thought, for here He had spent His childhood.

Colorful rag rugs hanging out to dry on the deeply recessed, shadowy balconies in Nazareth.

There are many who follow the trade of Joseph the Carpenter in present-day Nazareth, and some of them have their workshops on Joseph Street.

In old Nazareth, the city of Jesus, there are many grottoes under the existing buildings. In this one, Joseph, Mary, and Jesus are said to have lived after their flight from Egypt.

Bethlehem had been a serious city with many solemn memories. But Nazareth was a light and merry town, which echoed with the shrill cries of the streetmongers and the steady blows of the carpenters' hammers. Here the children were friendly and full of mischief.

IN THE VALLEY OF THE JORDAN

Up in the north, where Moses long ago first caught sight of the snow-covered summit of Mt. Hermon, after his journey through the desert, is the source of the river Jordan. In its deep valley, which lies several hundred feet

below sea level, the Jordan flows through the Huleh Marshes, now drained, on through the Sea of Galilee, and down to the Dead Sea near Jericho. The river valley is fertile, but on both sides of it stretches the desert.

It was in this river that the prophet John the Baptist baptized Jesus. Thus the Jordan became one of the best-known rivers in the whole world.

When Pia came to the river, she was almost disappointed in it, so small and insignificant it seemed. From where she stood, the Jordan was simply a slow-moving stream, not very deep and scented spicily by the eucalyptus trees along its banks. It was not at all the mighty river she

The richest catches in the Sea of Gennesaret consist partly of St. Peter's fish, a spotted fish similar to the haddock, and partly of fresh-water sardines, which resemble Baltic herring. They are both quite delicious.

Isaskar and Elia are the names of these fishermen. Their boat is the same kind as those used on the Sea of Galilee for thousands of years.

had imagined it would be. In a nearby bush she saw a chameleon just changing color. Stalking about at the edge of the water were solemn silver-white herons, and gleaming kingfishers flashed above the mirror-smooth surface of the stream. As Pia thrust a reed into the water, the crabs, like mighty spiders, scuttled away.

The Sea of Gennesaret, the Sea of Tiberias, the Sea of Galilee — this body of water has had many names. "And Jesus, walking by the sea of Galilee, saw two brethren, Simon called Peter, and Andrew his brother, casting a net into the sea; for they were fishers." (*Matthew 4:18*) Thus it reads in the Bible. Even today fishing is carried on there. Pia saw many fishermen casting their red nylon nets into the Sea of Galilee from boats that still look as they did in the time of Jesus. And they could catch a lot of fish! When the nets were pulled in, they glistened as if they were filled with silver coins. Instead, they were filled with thousands of fresh-water sardines. Men, women, and children — the young and the old — along the shores and on floats farther out on the water took the fish from the nets, to be sold later in Haifa, Tel Aviv, Jerusalem, and other cities.

On the outskirts of the fishing village of Tiberias, at one time the most important Jewish city after the fall of Jerusalem, there are hot springs, which for many thousands of years have been famous for their healing powers.

Pia knelt down and traced with her finger the outline of the basket and the fishes.

The ancient earthenware jar, which holds over eighty quarts, is said to be one of those that Jesus used at the marriage in Cana in changing water to wine.

According to legend, demons, at the command of King Solomon, caused the ordinary cold springs to become hot. People no longer believe in demons, but the warm water of the springs can still be of benefit to the sick.

On the shore of the Sea of Galilee, at the place where Jesus once fed five thousand people with five loaves and two fishes, a church has been built in recent times. Before then, an earlier church had stood there from which a mosaic floor still remains. Pia looked in wonder at the basket with the loaves and the two fishes that still show in faded colors on this old, old floor.

Above and below right: Shepherds still tend their flocks of black goats and white sheep on the stony, sun-drenched hillsides of northern Galilee.

Right: In the Valley of the Shadow of Death, between Jerusalem and Jericho, lies a hermitage. Many hermits live in the caves surrounding the cloister.

A few miles from Tiberias and the Sea of Galilee is the little Arabian village of Cana, where Jesus worked His first miracle. In the Franciscan Church there, Pia saw a large stone jar — just such a one as Jesus might have used long ago. The water that Jesus turned into wine at the marriage in Cana came from the stream under the floor where the jug was placed.

Later, among the shepherds who tended their flocks on the stony hillsides, Pia said farewell to Galilee, the country of Jesus' childhood and early youth, and traveled southward.

THE WALLS OF JERICHO

Several thousand years ago the city of Jericho was strongly fortified with walls around it. One time, the Bible tells us, when the city was besieged, war trumpets sounded and the walls came tumbling down. The ruins of these walls have been dug out of the grass-covered hills.

Jericho is now a small, insignificant place, chiefly a town for tourists and archaeologists. After Pia had searched for a while among the piles of gravel, her pockets were filled with bits of earthenware urns used to hold oil and water.

Near Jericho rises the Mountain of Temptation, where Satan tempted Jesus by showing Him all the lands of the

Right: Women at the well. The Arab women fetch water every day, and it is really their only opportunity to meet and talk together.

Left: On these foundations the walls of Jericho — one of the world's oldest-known cities — once stood, only to fall when the battle trumpets sounded.

world in their beauty. From this mountain you can see a fertile green valley irrigated by the river Jordan, which not far from here flows into the Dead Sea.

Old Jerusalem with the Mount of Olives in the background. Today only Arabs live there.

In the Garden of Gethsemane, herbs bloom the year around and centuries-old olive trees offer shade and coolness.

From the Garden of Gethsemane, Jesus was led away to be examined by the high priest, Caiaphas. This stairway leads to the place where the palace of the high priest once stood.

A section of the Via Dolorosa, the road Jesus followed as He carried the cross from Pilate's house to Golgotha.

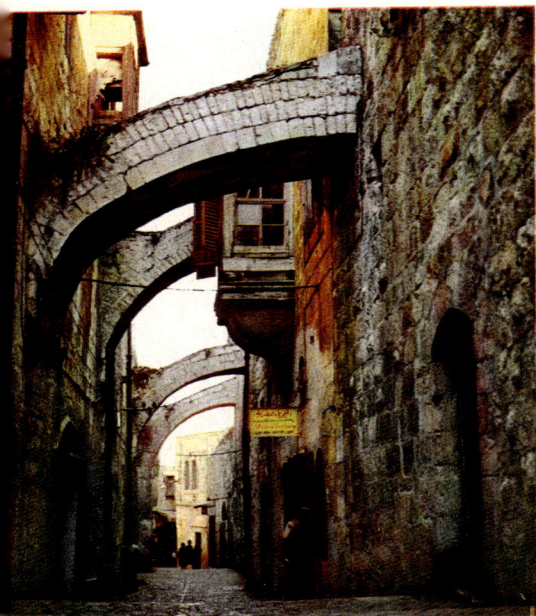

JERUSALEM

Outside the walls of the old part of Jerusalem, cars were speeding along broad, modern streets, but inside the walls Pia had to elbow her way through dark, narrow alleys. She was jostled by pack donkeys, by the poor but colorfully dressed people, by monks and nuns, and by tourists eagerly taking pictures. Strange smells filled the air. Outside the shops, tables were piled high with fruits, animal carcasses, rolls of gaudy cloth, and old shoes. Carpets and blankets, copper vessels, kerosene stoves, rags and scrap iron were spread on the pavement. Cries echoed between the stone walls; a guide took Pia by the arm and offered his services. Throngs of children were at play; donkey drivers shouted; and sheep bleated. Pia had landed right in the middle of an Eastern bazaar.

So this was Jerusalem. And this was what a holy city looked like! After the pushing and shoving, Pia was almost tired enough for tears, but the friendly monks of the Greek Orthodox Church came to her rescue. They let her rest in the cloister until she was ready to set out again.

It was hard for Pia to find her way in the old Jerusalem, the city within the walls. Sometimes she took the wrong turning on the winding streets, which often rose or fell steeply or changed into narrow stairways.

Once she found herself wedged in among a group of tourists in the temple square. This was where King

At the present time, the site of Jesus' tomb is a low, narrow crypt lighted by flickering candles, deep inside the Church of the Holy Sepulchre.

Solomon, thousands of years ago, had built a great temple, its gates and walls covered with gold. It had been destroyed long since.

Jerusalem was like no other city Pia had ever seen. She watched a procession on the Via Dolorosa, the Way of the Cross. It was a procession of Christians, following the path that Jesus once followed on his way up to Golgotha. At the head of it, a man staggered under the burden of a huge cross.

Jerusalem was like a great meeting place for people from every country, Christians and Mohammedans alike. But the Wailing Wall of the Jews stood deserted. The people of Israel no longer have access to the holy places in old Jerusalem. It belongs to another country — to Jordan — and the Jews must content themselves by looking at the holy places from the top of Mount Zion, which, like a great boundary marker, rises between the old Jerusalem and the new, which is the modern capital of Israel.

In the orthodox Jewish school in Jerusalem, only boys are given instruction. They must wear skull caps or hats during the lessons.

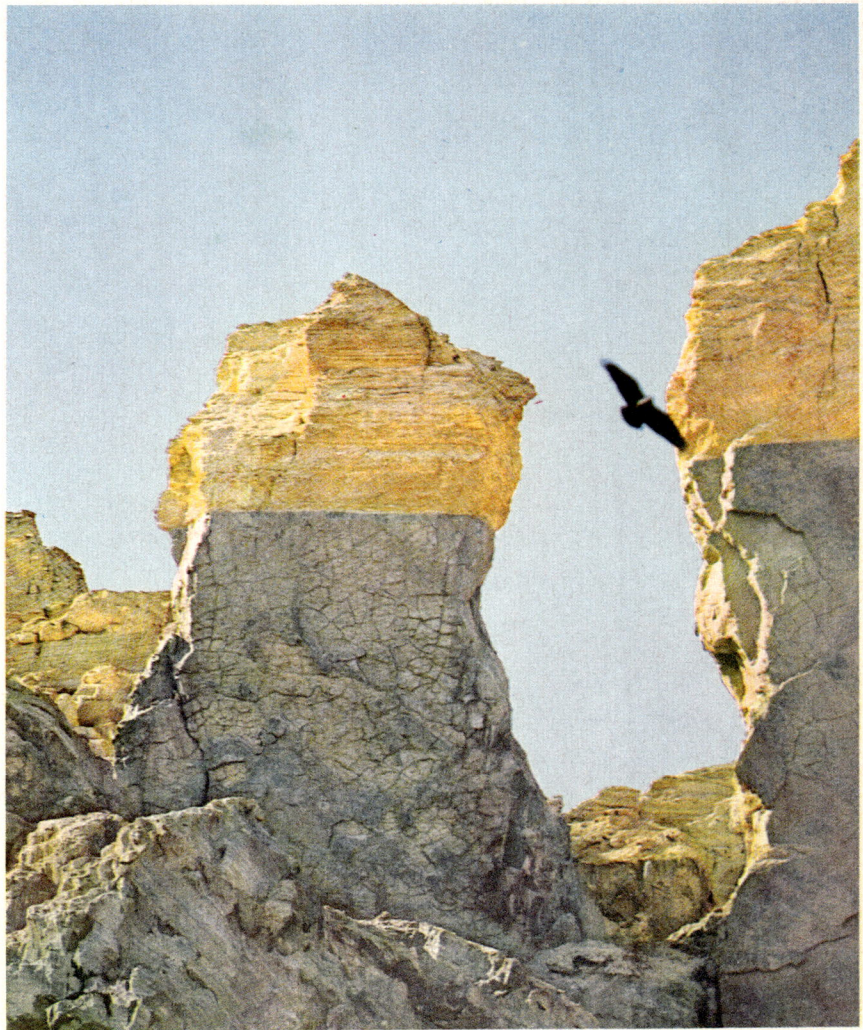

Salt mountains rise all around the shores of the Dead Sea. One of them is called "Lot's Wife," after the woman who was turned into a pillar of salt when she turned around to view the destruction of Sodom and Gomorrah. (*Genesis 19:26*)

Left: The Dead Sea lies about 1,300 feet below sea level and is the lowest point on the surface of the earth. Its water is so salty that it is difficult to swim — your hands and feet are simply forced up out of the water.

THE DEAD SEA

The Dead Sea! Pia had always thought the name sounded almost frightening. And its other name — the Salt Sea — wasn't a great deal better. She knew that there was no life to be found in this sea (47 miles long and over 1,000 feet deep) — not a fish, not even a single water plant. Salt and sun had burned away all living things.

When she arrived at the shore, near the place where the city of Sodom had stood long ago, she looked with curiosity at the blue-green water rippling in the gentle breeze.

There was not a reed in sight — only rocks and stones as far as she could see. On the opposite shore lay the Mountains of Moab, misty in the sun haze over the lake. Pia put on her new red bathing suit and made her way carefully over the salt sand to the water. It was shallow. Did she dare go in? The water felt so strange, and when she tasted it, her tongue burned bitterly.

Finally, she lay on her back, and she floated — just as easily as a cork! Wherever she looked, she saw the cold, dead-looking mountains. Yes, the Salt Sea had probably always been dead, but she was no longer frightened by the name. As she left the water and went to take a shower, salt crystals glistened on her entire body.

The road leading northward from Sodom, along the western shore of the Dead Sea, seemed to be no more than a camel path, but it was possible to drive a jeep on it. Here and there Pia noticed hot sulfur springs. She saw, too, that the ground was covered with spiny mounds — bushes that sometimes were rooted in the earth and sometimes were tumbled in the wind. The branches, yellowish-brown and quite dry, were used as camel fodder, Pia was surprised to learn.

Their necks outstretched, a fleet of camels sways along the dry, stony shore of the Dead Sea in search of water.

The friendly, smiling camel drivers wear cloth around their heads as a protection against sand, salt, and sun.

From a spring in the mountains, water is piped down to the village of Ein Gede, where Jewish settlers now raise crops of vegetables and fruit the year around.

THE DESERT BLOOMS

A long distance from the Dead Sea, in the Negev Desert, which lies in the southernmost part of Israel, Pia paid a visit to a "kibbutz," a community of farmers, called Yotvata. Everywhere thousands of flowers bloomed brilliantly — huge gladioli, red, yellow, white, and purple — but just a few hundred yards from the lovely flower fields lay drifts of powdery sand. Ceaseless toil and irrigation had changed the desert into a flowering oasis. Green

A young Jewish girl helps to pick vegetables in Ein Gede during the busy season. It is unbelievably warm there and, consequently, hard to hire workers. Scouts and other youth organizations pitch camps in the neighborhood and help out.

borders of eucalyptus trees and mimosa protected the fields from sandstorms.

For many hundreds of years man struggled for existence in this barren land, working with primitive tools. Now there are modern inventions to help him. From pumping stations on the surrounding heights, water runs down in shallow ditches, which cross the plains like narrow blue ribbons. Everywhere Pia saw teams of people at work — men digging, two by two, in the sandy earth and thrusting olive tree plants into the holes.

Pia went even farther south in the Negev. There, where

In the huge sandbox of the desert... Fine-grained sand to sift through your fingers — sand that is lifted and carried great distances by the wind.

But the sand can blossom. Huge bunches of gladioli are tied up and sent by air to Europe in the winter.

Israel narrows to a point leading to the Red Sea's Gulf of Aqaba, there are red mountains that are rich in copper. King Solomon used slaves, thousands of years ago, to work the mines. Now machines do all the work.

Leaving the desert, Pia took a plane trip diagonally across most of the Holy Land. The little city of Caesarea was her destination. In the time of Jesus it was an important harbor with many splendid buildings. Archaeologists have made excavations here and have found the foundations of many old houses, as well as many enormous white-marble statues.

During her travels up and down and across the Holy
Land, Pia made new friends everywhere. Young people
of her own age often gave her little presents — a few
oranges, perhaps an old coin, a flower, or some other
small souvenir. In Acre, an ancient seaport north of Caesarea, she met three friendly schoolgirls, all of whom
came from different countries. One was from Morocco,

The olive tree, the tree of peace, is one of the first things to be planted in the desert. The plant has to be fastened down with ropes to keep it from being tumbled about by the sandstorms.

Once long ago King Solomon's slaves mined copper out of the red rocks in the south of the Negev Desert. Today there is a modern copper company that gets its ore out of the same mountains.

Left: In 1955, archaeologists unearthed this huge white-marble statue in Caesarea, a harbor city during the time of the Roman Empire.

Left: In the Negev Desert, about twelve miles from the Egyptian-Sinai border, lies the ruined city of Subeita, which flourished in the Byzantine Era about 1,500 years ago. The city has three churches. These are the ruins of the largest.

Right: The waves of the Mediterranean beat against the ruins of Caesarea. From this city St. Paul set out on his second missionary journey, which spread Christianity to Europe.

New life in an old city. The city of Acre, north of Haifa on the Mediterranean, has a long and great history. The generals of Alexander the Great fought here. Here the Crusaders advanced, and here Napoleon dreamed of conquering India.

another from Algeria, and the third from Poland. They and their parents had not been in Israel very long, but in spite of the fact that all of the girls spoke different languages, they had no difficulty in understanding one another. Pia joined them in playing dolls and hopscotch. Games are much the same the world over.

AMONG THE BEDOUINS

After a journey of only a few hours from the flowering desert, Pia reached a wild, untamed part of the land where people still live as they did in Old Testament times. She was invited to visit the sheik, Aud Abu Muamer, who lived near the city of Abraham and Isaac — Beer-sheba, or the Seven Wells. The sheik met her outside his grayish-brown tent. He wore a European suit, but over it a gray cloak reaching all the way to his feet, and on his head a snow-white cloth with black bands. He led Pia to the entrance of the tent, where she took off her sandals, following the custom of the country, before stepping on the colorful carpets inside. Soon she was settled comfortably on the cushions inside the tent and welcomed with a glass of sweet tea.

Crossing the desert on the way to the Bedouin section of Israel.

The sheik's son, who was grinding coffee in honor of Pia's arrival, struck the coffee mortar with extra force in order to let the tribe know of her arrival. Inside and outside the tent, a great many Bedouins assembled. The sound of words in Arabic buzzed in Pia's ears, and wherever she looked, she saw smiling, happy faces.

The slopes of this weather-beaten mountain look as if a stream of molten gold had hardened on its way down. It was in this area that the children of Israel wandered so long in the wilderness.

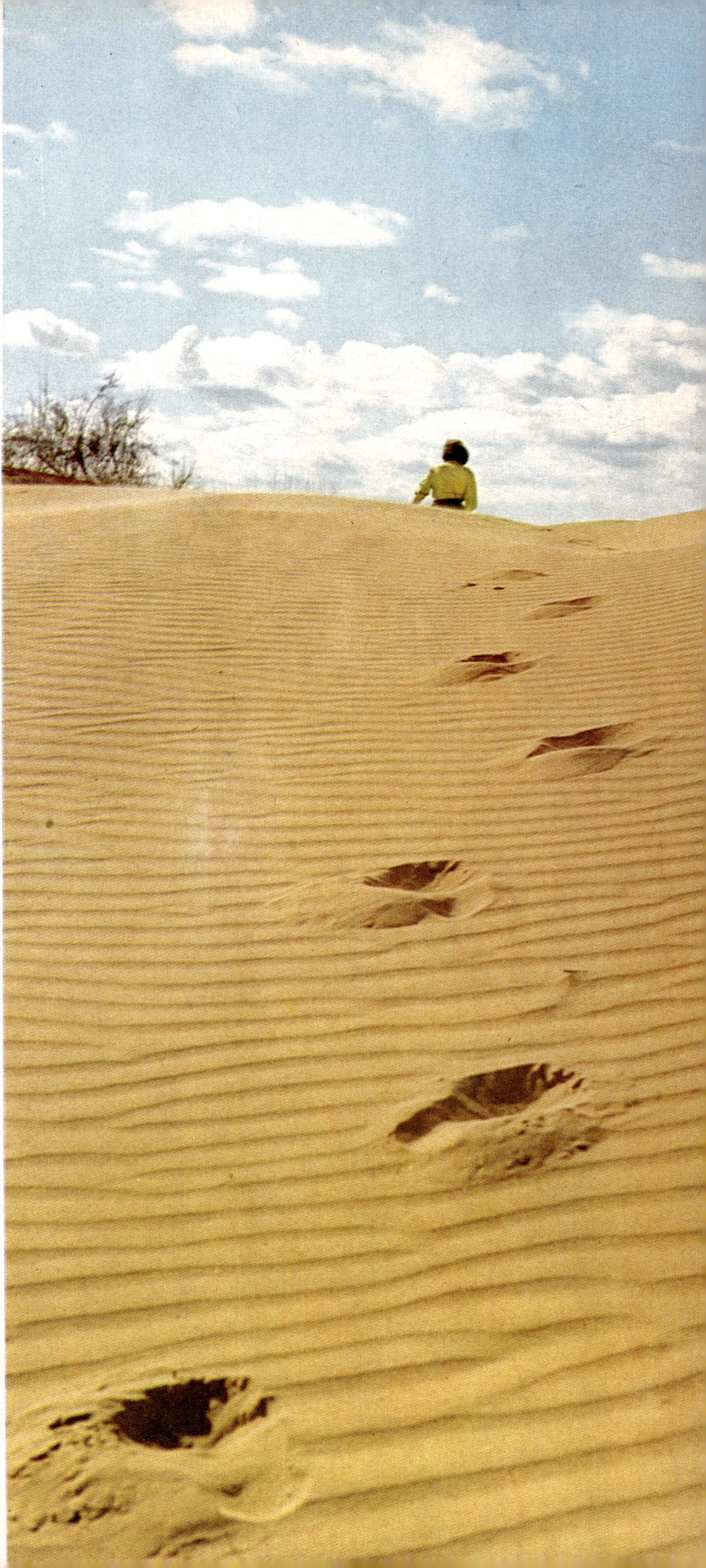

At most places in the desert only the wind leaves traces in the sand. The wind can move sand dunes for miles through the desert, thus threatening to bury the flowering oases.

Achmed, the eight-year-old son of the sheik, grinds coffee in the beautifully ornamented clay mortar. The rhythmic beats against the mortar announce that the encampment has been honored with guests from afar.

For thousands of years seeds have been ground between flat oval stones.

Music, played on a one-stringed instrument, the rebab, in honor of the guests.

Word has gone forth over the dunes of the desert, and the Bedouins have arrived — on foot, on camels, horses, and donkeys. Deep inside the shelter of the tent sit the sheik and his son, and beside them the leader of the camp; ordinary men must sit outside in the desert sun.

As the sun set, turning the sand dunes into mounds of gold, Pia looked out over the desert. What a strange and wonderful country this was — a new country, bustling with life, cultivated with the help of tractors and irrigation systems, but also an ancient land where time stood still, where camels swayed through the desert just as they had done for thousands of years. Yes, it was a holy land — where, beyond the desert sands, there were oases and sources of water and the promise of a rich future.